the Pocket Guide to the
glucose
revolution
and losing weight

KAYE FOSTER-POWELL
DR JENNIE BRAND MILLER • DR STEPHEN COLAGIURI

D1343561

CORONET BOOKS
Hodder & Stoughton

Copyright © 1998 by Kaye Foster-Powell, Janette Brand Miller and
Dr Stephen Colagiuri

The right of Kaye Foster-Powell, Janette Brand Miller and Dr
Stephen Colagiuri to be identified as the Authors of
the Work has been asserted by them in accordance with the
Copyright, Designs and Patents Act 1988.

First published in Australia in 1998 by
Hodder Headline Australia Pty Limited

First published in Great Britain in 2000
by Hodder and Stoughton
A division of Hodder Headline
A Coronet Paperback

This United Kingdom edition is published by arrangement with
Hodder Headline Australia Pty Limited
A Coronet Paperback

10 9 8 7 6 5 4 3 2 1

A CIP catalogue record for this title is available from the
British Library

ISBN 0 340 76991 2

Printed and bound in Great Britain by
Omnia Books Ltd, Glasgow

Hodder and Stoughton
A division of Hodder Headline
338 Euston Road
London NW1 3BH

FOREWORD

There are many people in Britain and the Republic of Ireland who are overweight or even obese. The latest figures show that more than 50 per cent of adult men and women are overweight and/or obese. While the health cost of such figures is acknowledged, the personal cost and anguish of being overweight is often underestimated. Many people spend lots of time, effort and money trying to get or keep their weight down. The figures also show how in Britain, as in Australia, we are failing. Despite a multitude of published diets, ways and opportunities to exercise, we continue to put on weight. Individually we need to eat the things we like and that are best for us through the various stages of life. We must also learn to choose wisely from the abundance of foods that are available.

This *Pocket Guide to the Glucose Revolution and Losing Weight* is timely. It talks about foods, and does not concentrate on Calories or individual constituents of foods. This approach to eating allows you to be satisfied, eat foods you enjoy and be healthy. It helps weight loss and is the sort of eating necessary to help maintain weight. Of course, increasing your daily activity is important as well. The authors have wide experience in nutrition and the health consequences of being overweight, yet they all know the difficulties of dieting. Their nutritional knowledge, their understanding of people and of what is necessary to lose weight and keep it off are obvious.

I commend this book and its approach to eating. It is sensible, deals with foods and allows choice. It is based on the latest scientific knowledge and is a practical approach to the problem of being overweight, both for the individual and for society at large. Try it and see for yourself.

Professor Ian Caterson MBBS, Bsc (Med), PhD, FRACP
Boden Professor of Human Nutrition
University of Sydney, NSW

CONTENTS

THERE'S NO NEED TO FEEL HUNGRY WHEN YOU NEED TO LOSE WEIGHT

When you use the G.I. factor as the basis for your food choices, there is:

■ no need to overly restrict your food intake

■ no need to obsessively count Calories

■ no need to starve yourself

INTRODUCTION

When it comes to what to eat to lose weight, it is not simply a matter of reducing how much you eat. Research in Britain and Australia has shown that the type of food you give your body determines what fuel it's going to burn and what it's going to store as body fat. It has also revealed that certain foods are much more satisfying than others. This is where the G.I. factor comes to the fore. Low G.I. foods have two very special advantages for people wanting to lose weight:

■ they fill you up and keep you satisfied for longer
■ they help you burn more of your body fat and less of your body muscle

The G.I. factor (glycaemic index) of foods is simply a ranking of foods based on their immediate effect on blood sugar levels.

■ Carbohydrate foods that break down quickly during digestion have the highest G.I. factors. Their blood sugar response is fast and high
■ Carbohydrates which break down slowly, releasing glucose gradually into the blood stream, have low G.I. factors

If you are trying to lose weight, foods with a low G.I. factor will help you:

- increase your food intake without increasing your waistline
- control your appetite
- choose the right amount of carbohydrate and the right sort of carbohydrate for your lifestyle and your wellbeing

If you are overweight (or consider yourself overweight) chances are that you have looked at countless books, brochures and magazines offering a solution to losing weight. New diets or miracle weight-loss solutions seem to appear weekly. They are clearly good for selling magazines, but for the majority of people who are overweight the 'diets' don't work (if they did, there wouldn't be so many!).

At best, (while you stick to it), a 'diet' may reduce your Calorie intake. At its worst, a 'diet' may change your body composition for the fatter. That is because many diets employ the technique of reducing your carbohydrate intake to bring about quick weight loss. The weight you lose, however, is mostly water (that was trapped or held with stored carbohydrate) and eventually muscle (as it is broken down to produce glucose).

It is possible that, once you return to your former way of eating, you regain a little bit more fat. With each desperate repetition of a diet you lose more muscle. Over years, the resultant change in body composition to less muscle and more fat which may occur in some people makes it increasingly difficult to lose weight.

WHY EXERCISE KEEPS YOU MOVING

The effect of exercise doesn't stop when you stop moving. People who exercise have higher metabolic rates and their bodies burn more Calories per minute, even when they are asleep!

THIS BOOK IS NOT ANOTHER DIET!

This book brings you the scientific evidence about control of body weight and how the G.I. factor can be used to best support your efforts at weight loss.

- ■ We show you how to put the G.I. factor into practice.
- ■ We provide practical hints for changing your eating habits.
- ■ We give a week of low G.I. low Calorie menus plus a nutritional analysis for each menu and its G.I. factor.
- ■ We include an A-Z listing of over 300 foods with their G.I. factor, carbohydrate and fat content.

WHAT IS THE G.I. FACTOR?

The G.I. factor is a scientifically validated tool in the dietary management of diabetes, weight reduction and athletic performance.

Originally, research into the glycaemic index of foods was inspired by the desire to identify the best foods for people with diabetes. But scientists are now discovering that the glycaemic index has implications for everyone.

Eating to lose weight with low G.I. foods is easier because you don't have to go hungry and what you end up with is true fat release.

The real aim in losing weight is losing body fat. Perhaps it would be better described as 'releasing' body fat? After all, to lose something, suggests that you hope to find it again some day!

The G.I. factor is a ranking of foods based on their overall effects on blood sugar levels

---

IS YOUR WEIGHT A PROBLEM?

In putting together a book for weight loss we are only too well aware of the pressure many people feel to lose weight. We don't intend to add to that pressure. In fact we suggest you clarify in your own mind whether your weight really is a problem to you.

It's worth doing an assessment of your situation to clarify your goals as far as your body weight goes.

Here are some questions you need to ask yourself.

■ Are you overfat?
■ Is your weight contributing to poor health?
■ Is your weight impacting on your daily life?
■ Do you really want to lose weight?
■ Why are you overweight?

Are you an apple or a pear?
Your waist circumference should be less than
90 cm (women) or less than 100 cm (men).

ARE YOU OVERFAT?

A weight-for-height chart can show you a range of weights that is considered healthiest for your height, but these charts are not appropriate for everyone. People from different populations around the world cannot always be compared on the same scale. Asian people tend to be smaller (lighter and shorter) than Pacific Islanders for example. Rugby league players appear heavy in proportion to their height because of their muscle bulk. This doesn't mean they are unhealthy. A large mass of body fat on the other hand, is associated with health risk. This is so, particularly when the fat is centrally located. That means around the central part of your body – waist, tummy, abdomen. Women often carry a lot of fat on their hips, thighs, buttocks, giving them a pear shape. This fat is an energy store for reproduction and carries little health risk. You can tell if you have too much fat on your middle by measuring your waist with a tape measure. A waist circumference bigger than 90 cm (females) or 100 cm (males) is too big.

IS YOUR WEIGHT CONTRIBUTING TO YOUR POOR HEALTH?

Centrally located fat is associated with a range of health problems. Among these are heart disease, diabetes, high blood pressure, gout, gallstones, sleep apnoea (snoring) and arthritis. It is thought that even if your fat is more uniformly distributed, it may affect your health by limiting your physical mobility, creating strain and pain in your joints, causing you to puff and pant with any physical exertion.

For the majority of people who are overweight, magazine 'miracle diets' don't work. If they did, there wouldn't be so many of them.

IS YOUR WEIGHT HAVING AN IMPACT ON YOUR DAILY LIFE?

Aside from the physical side effects of being overweight, there are an equal number of emotional and psychological consequences. Your weight may inhibit you from meeting people, reduce your self esteem, make you feel ugly, stop you from going swimming, make shopping for clothes a nightmare, stop you playing with your children, prevent you from playing sport ...

It is generally no fun being overweight.

If you eat healthy foods most of the time, with the occasional indulgence, and do physical activity for at least 30 minutes 4–5 times a week, then your size and shape may be right for you.

DO YOU REALLY WANT TO LOSE WEIGHT?

The proportion of overweight people in our society is increasing, despite the expanding weight-loss industry and an ever increasing range of 'diet' or 'lite' foods. It is clear that the answer to preventing people from becoming overweight is not a simple one. Nor is losing weight easy to do. The G.I. factor, however, makes it that little bit easier for you because it tells you which foods satisfy hunger for longer, and are the least likely to make you fat. When you use the G.I. factor as the basis for your food choices:

■ there is no need to overly restrict your food intake
■ there is no need to obsessively count Calories
■ there is no need to starve yourself

Learning which foods your body works best on, is what using the G.I. factor is all about.

It is worthwhile taking control over aspects of your lifestyle that have an impact on your weight. You may not create a new body from your efforts, but you will feel better about the body you've got. Eating and exercising for your best performance is the aim of the game.

WHY ARE YOU OVERWEIGHT?

Consider the energy balance paradox that exists in our bodies. Many people, without much conscious effort, maintain a steady body weight. This is despite huge variations in how much they eat. For a proportion of people who are gaining weight, this apparent balancing of energy intake and output, seems lost or inoperative. So, despite every fad diet, every exercise program, even operations and medications, body weight can steadily increase over the years, regardless of all apparent efforts to control it.

There is a genetic predisposition to weight gain in some people. A child born to overweight parents is much more likely to be overweight than one whose parents were not overweight, for example. Studies in twins also provide evidence that our body weight and shape is at least partially determined by our genes.

Identical twins tend to be similar in body weight even if they are raised apart. Even twins adopted out as infants show the body-fat profile of their true parents rather than that of their adoptive parents. These findings suggest that our genes are a stronger determinant of weight than our environment (which includes the food we eat).

It seems that information stored in our genes governs our tendency to store Calories as either fat or as lean muscle tissue. Overfeeding a large group of identical twins confirmed that within each pair, weight gain was similar. However the amount of weight gained between sets of identical twins varied greatly. From this, researchers concluded that our genes control the way our bodies respond to overeating. Some sets of twins gained a lot of weight, while others gained only a little, even though all were overconsuming an equivalent amount of excess Calories.

All this isn't to say that if your parents were overweight, you should resign yourself to being overweight. But it may help you understand why you have to watch your weight while other people seemingly don't have to watch theirs.

So, if you were born with a tendency to be overweight, why does it matter what you eat? The answer is that foods (or more correctly, nutrients) are not equal in their effect on body weight. In particular the way the body responds to dietary fat makes matters worse. If you are overweight it is likely that the amount of fat you burn is small, relative to the amount of fat you store. Consequently, the more fat you eat, the more fat you store. Although this may sound logical, the 'eat-more, store-more' mechanism does not exist for all nutrients.

Amongst all four major sources of Calories in food, (protein, fat, carbohydrate and alcohol), fat is unique. When we increase our intake of protein, alcohol or carbohydrate the body's response is to burn more of that particular energy source. Sensibly, the body matches the supply of fuel with the type of fuel burned. A fundamental difference between fat and carbohydrate is that fat tends to be stored whereas carbohydrate has a tendency to be burned. If your carbohydrate intake is low, it may reduce the amount of Calories you burn each day by 5 to 10 per cent.

While you may not have been born owning the best set of genes for the current environment, you can still influence your weight by the lifestyle choices you make. The message is simply this: if you believe that you are at risk of being overweight, you should think seriously about minimising fat and eating more carbohydrate.

Despite genetic predisposition weight gain can only result from an imbalance of energy in and energy out. In this regard, we know that obesity is a multifactorial disorder – increased food intake, declining physical activity, genetics, aging, a high fat diet – they all play a part. But what it all boils down to is that if we take in too much (overeat) and don't burn up enough (don't exercise) we are likely to put on weight.

MEASURING THE FUEL WE NEED

Calories are a measure of the fuel we need. Our bodies need a certain number of Calories every day to work, just as a car needs so many litres of petrol to be driven a certain distance. Food and drink are our source of Calories. If we eat and drink too much, we may store the extra Calories as body fat. If we consume fewer Calories than we need, our bodies will break down their stores of fat to make up for the shortfall.

FACTORS INFLUENCING YOUR BODY WEIGHT

Consider which of the following factors may play a role for you.

■ **Total food intake**

Do you eat too much food?

■ **The balance of different nutrients**

Do you eat a healthy, balanced diet?

■ **Energy expenditure associated with movement**

How much do you move in a normal day?

■ **Energy expenditure associated with physical activity**

How much planned activity do you do?

■ **Resting metabolic rate**

How much fuel does your body burn at rest?

■ **Thermic response to food**

How much fuel does your body waste as heat?

■ **A body's preference to store excess Calories as either fat or muscle**

Do you have more fat or muscle?

METABOLISM

Our genetic make-up also underlies our metabolism, (basically how many Calories we burn per minute). Bodies, like cars, differ in this regard. A V-8 consumes more fuel to run than a small 4-cylinder car. A bigger body, generally, requires more Calories than a smaller one. Everybody has a **resting metabolic rate**. This is a measure of the amount of Calories our bodies use when we are at rest. When a car is stationary, the engine idles – using just enough fuel to keep the motor running. When we are asleep, our engine keeps running (for example, our heart keeps beating) and we use a minimum number of Calories. This is our resting metabolic rate.

When we start exercising, or even just moving around, the number of Calories, or the amount of fuel we use, increases. However, the largest amount (around 70 per cent) of the Calories used in a 24-hour period, are those used to maintain our basic body functioning.

Since our resting metabolic rate is where most of the Calories we eat are used, it is a significant determinant of our body weight. The lower your resting energy expenditure, the greater your risk of gaining weight, and vice versa. We all know someone who appears to 'eat like a horse' but is positively thin! Almost in awe we comment on their 'fast metabolism', and we may not be far off the mark!

FOOD AND BODY BASICS

What foods do cause people to become overweight?

It was widely (and wrongly) believed for many years, that sugar and starchy foods like potato, rice and pasta were the cause of obesity. Twenty years ago, every diet for weight loss advocated restriction of these carbohydrate-rich foods. One of the reasons for this carbohydrate restriction stemmed from the 'instant results' of low carbohydrate diets. If your diet is very low in carbohydrate, you will lose weight. The problem is that what you primarily lose is fluid, and not fat. What's more, a low carbohydrate diet depletes the glycogen stores in the muscles thus making exercise difficult and tiring.

Sugar has been blamed as a cause of people becoming overweight primarily because it is often found in high fat foods, where it serves to make the fat more palatable and tempting. Chocolate, which contains almost one-third of its weight in the form of fat, would be fairly unpalatable without the sugar.

Current thinking is that there is little evidence to condemn sugar or starchy foods as the cause of people becoming overweight. Overweight people show a preference for fat-containing foods rather than a preference for foods high in sugar. In a survey performed at the University of Michigan where obese men and women listed their favourite foods, men listed mainly meats (protein-fat sources) and women listed mainly cakes, biscuits, doughnuts (combinations of carbohydrate-fat sources). Other studies have found that obese people habitually consume a higher fat diet than people who have a healthy weight. So, it appears that a higher intake of fatty food is strongly related to the development of obesity – not carbohydrate-rich foods.

COUNTING THE CALORIES IN OUR NUTRIENTS

All foods contain Calories. Often the Calorie content of a food is considered a measure of how fattening it is. Of all the nutrients in food that we consume, carbohydrate yields the fewest Calories per gram.

carbohydrate	4 calories per gram
protein	4 Calories per gram
alcohol	7 Calories per gram
fat	9 Calories per gram

Whether you are going to gain weight from eating a particular food really depends on how much that food adds to your total Calorie intake in relation to how much you burn up.

To lose weight you need to eat fewer Calories and burn more Calories. If your total Calorie balance does not change—there will be no change in your weight. People who consume a high fat diet, tend to eat a high Calorie diet, because fatty foods yield more Calories for the same weight of food than carbohydrate foods. This is why substituting low-fat foods for high fat foods and a focus on reducing your total fat intake has the most potential to reduce your Calorie intake.

DID YOU KNOW?

The body loves to store fat. It is a way of protecting us in case of famine. In the midst of plenty we are building up our fat stores.

HOW CAN THE G.I. FACTOR HELP?

One of the toughest aspects of trying to lose weight can be feeling hungry all the time. But a gnawing, empty feeling isn't necessary when you are losing weight. Carbohydrates are natural appetite suppressants. Gram for gram of carbohydrate, those with a low G.I. factor are the most filling and prevent hunger pangs for longer.

In the past, it was believed that protein, fat and carbohydrate foods, taken in equal quantities, satisfy our appetite equally. We now know from recent research that the satiating (making us feel full) capacity of these three nutrients is not equal.

Fatty foods, in particular, have only a weak effect on satisfying appetite relative to the number of Calories they provide. In an experimental situation, volunteers will consistently over-consume Calories if the foods they are offered are high in fat. When high carbohydrate and low-fat foods are offered, they consume fewer Calories, eating to appetite. So, carbohydrate foods are the best for satisfying your appetite without over satisfying your Calorie requirement.

In studies conducted at the University of Sydney, people were given a range of individual foods that contained equal numbers of Calories, then the satiety (feeling of fullness and satisfaction after eating) responses were compared. The researchers found that the most filling foods were foods high in carbohydrate that contained fewer Calories per gram. This included potatoes, porridge, apples, oranges and pasta. Eating more of these foods satisfies appetite without providing excess Calories. On the other hand, high fat foods that provide a lot of Calories per gram, like croissants, chocolate and peanuts, were the least satisfying. These foods help you store more fat and are less filling to eat.

Many people notice that eating extra carbohydrate at a meal tends to be compensated by eating less food at the next meal. When we eat more carbohydrate, the body responds by increasing its production of glycogen. Glycogen is stored as glucose, the critical fuel for our brain and muscles. The size of these stores is limited, however, and they must be continuously refilled by carbohydrate from the diet. Good glycogen stores ensure a well-fuelled body and make it easier to exercise. Even when we are not exercising, the body will use carbohydrate in preference to other fuel sources, because it is attempting to match the source of Calories to the type of Calories used.

By eating a high carbohydrate diet you will tend to automatically lower your fat intake, and by choosing your carbohydrate from low G.I. foods, you make it even more satisfying.

What's more, even when the Calorie intake is the same,

people eating low G.I. foods may lose more weight than those eating high G.I. foods. In a South African study, the investigators divided overweight volunteers into two groups: one group ate high G.I. foods and the other, low G.I. foods. The amount of Calories, fat, protein, carbohydrate and fibre in the diet was the same for both groups. Only the G.I. factor of the diets was different. The low G.I. group included foods like lentils, pasta, porridge and corn in their diet and excluded high G.I. foods like potato and white bread. After 12 weeks, the volunteers in the group eating low G.I. foods had lost, on average, 9 kilograms – 2 kilograms more than people in the group eating the diet of high G.I. foods.

How did the low G.I. diet work? The most significant finding was the different effects of the two diets on the level of insulin in the blood. Low G.I. foods resulted in lower levels of insulin circulating in the bloodstream. Insulin is a hormone that is not only involved in regulating blood sugar levels, it also plays a key part in when and how we store fat. High levels of insulin often exist in obese people, in those with high blood fat levels (either cholesterol or triglyceride) and those with heart disease. This study suggested that the low insulin responses associated with low G.I. foods helped the body to burn more fat rather than store it.

If you are still fearful of gaining weight from eating

more pasta, bread and potatoes, consider this: the body actually has to use up Calories to convert the carbohydrate we eat into body fat. The cost is 23 per cent of the available Calories – that is, nearly one-quarter of the Calories of the carbohydrate are used up just storing it. Naturally, the body is not keen on wasting energy this way. In fact, the body converts carbohydrate to fat only under very unusual situations like forced overfeeding. The human body prefers the easy option. It is far more willing to add to our fat stores with the fat that we eat. Conversion of fat in food to body fat is an extremely efficient process and body fat stores are virtually limitless. No matter how excessive the amount of fat we eat, the body will always find space to store it.

A gnawing, empty feeling isn't necessary when you are losing weight because low G.I. foods are filling and prevent hunger pangs for longer.

WHICH FOODS ARE MOST FATTENING?

Let's compare two everyday foods which are almost 'pure' in the nutrition sense.

3 teaspoons of sugar   **versus**   1 teaspoon of butter
(almost pure carbohydrate)   (almost pure fat)

They contain virtually the same number of Calories.

46 Calories   versus   44 Calories

This means that you can eat three times the volume of sugar as you could butter for the same number of Calories! Look at these other examples:

■ A small grilled T-bone steak (about the size of a slice of bread) has the same Calories as 3 medium potatoes.

■ 3 slices of bread, thickly buttered, are equivalent to 6 slices of bread with no butter.

■ 3 chocolate cream biscuits have more Calories than a carton of low-fat chocolate milk.

■ Eating 1 piece of crumbed, fried chicken at lunch substitutes for the Calories of 6 slices of bread (without butter).

■ For every 1 cup of fried rice you eat you could eat 2 cups of boiled rice.

■ And if you're feeling extra hungry next time you stop for a coffee, consider that one slice of mudcake has the Calories of 4 slices of lightly buttered raisin toast!

In every case the highest fat foods have the highest Calorie count. Because carbohydrate has about half the Calories of fat, it is safer to eat more carbohydrate-rich food. What's more, your body is more likely to store fat and burn carbohydrate so the Calories contribute more to your 'spread' when they come from fat.

> *No matter how excessive*
> *the amount of fat we eat,*
> *the body will always find*
> *space to store it.*

YOU CAN EAT QUANTITY – JUST CONSIDER THE QUALITY!

Three tips for people trying to lose weight

1. Eat regular meals – include snacks in between if you are hungry.
2. Try to include a low G.I. food at every meal.
3. Ensure that your meals contain mainly carbohydrate, lean meat and vegetable foods and that the fat content is low.

> *Carbohydrates are natural appetite suppressants. And of all carbohydrate foods, those with a low G.I. factor are amongst the most filling and prevent hunger pangs for longer.*

EXERCISE – WE CAN'T LIVE WITHOUT IT

The number of overweight and obese people in our society is on the rise. Not surprising, you may think, given the abundance of foods available to us. We increasingly eat away from home and have a greater consumption of fast food and snack foods. But reported intakes of fat and Calories have, if anything, gone down! At the same time, however, a multitude of changes in living habits now mean that in both work and recreation we are more sedentary. Our physical activity levels are now so low that we have an imbalance in our energy equation where we don't burn up enough to account for the amount (albeit reduced) we eat.

To lose weight you need to eat fewer
Calories and burn more Calories – and
that means regular exercise and less
sedentary lifestyle.

THE BENEFITS OF EXERCISE

Most people could tell you at least one health benefit of exercise (reduces blood pressure, lowers the risk of heart disease, improves circulation, increases stamina, flexibility and strength) but the most motivating aspect of exercise is feeling so good about yourself for doing it.

Exercise speeds up our metabolic rate. By increasing our Calorie expenditure, exercise helps to balance our sometimes excessive Calorie intake from food.

Exercise makes our muscles better at using fat as a source of fuel. By improving the way insulin works, exercise increases the amount of fat we burn.

A low G.I. diet has the same effect. Low G.I. foods reduce the amount of insulin we need which makes fat easier to burn and harder to store. Since body fat is what you want to get rid of when you lose weight, exercise in combination with a low G.I. diet makes a lot of sense!

SO, WHAT CAN YOU DO TO GET MORE EXERCISE?

Getting more exercise doesn't necessarily mean daily aerobics classes and jogging around the block (although this is great if you want to do it). What it does mean is moving more in everyday living. It's the day-to-day things we do – shopping, ironing, chasing kids, walking from the station – where the bulk of our energy expenditure is. Since so much of our lifestyle is designed now to reduce our physical exertion it's become very important to catch bursts of physical activity wherever we can, to increase our energy output. It may mean using the stairs instead of the lift, taking a 10 minute walk at lunch time, walking to the shops to get the Sunday paper, hiding the remote control, parking a mile from work, or taking the dog for a walk each night. Also, have you ever thought of not using the car one day per week, or not watching TV for the whole of one day? Whatever it means, do it.

Besides increasing the incidental activity you will also benefit from some planned aerobic activity. This means activity that causes you to breathe more heavily and makes your heart beat faster. Walking, cycling, swimming, stair climbing are just a few examples. You'll need to accumulate a total of at least 30 minutes of this type of activity 5–6 days a week.

Remember that reduction in body weight takes time. Even after you've made changes in your exercise habits, your weight may not be any different on the scales. This is particularly true in women, whose bodies tend to adapt to increased Calorie expenditure.

Whatever it takes for you, do it. Regard movement as an opportunity to improve your physical well being and not an inconvenience.

Exercise makes our muscles better at using fat as a source of fuel.

WHY EXERCISE KEEPS YOU MOVING

The effect of exercise doesn't stop when you stop moving. People who exercise have higher metabolic rates and their bodies burn more Calories per minute even when they are asleep!

HOW TO MAKE YOUR EXERCISE SUCCESSFUL

Eight key factors to make exercise successful are:

- seeing a benefit for yourself
- enjoying what you do
- feeling that you can do it fairly well
- fitting it in with your daily life
- keeping it inexpensive
- making it accessible
- being safe
- being socially acceptable to your peers

DO YOU GET ALL THE NUTRIENTS YOU NEED?

To meet your average daily nutrient requirements you need to eat a certain amount of different types of foods. If you are trying to reduce your Calorie intake there is still a minimum amount of certain foods that you should be eating each day. These are:

■ **Breads/cereals/and grain foods – 5 servings or more**

1 serving means: 1 bowl breakfast cereal (30 grams)

    ½ cup cooked pasta or rice

    ½ cup cooked grain such as barley or wheat

    1 slice bread

    ½ bread roll or muffin

■ **Vegetables – 4 servings**

1 serving means: 1 medium potato (about 150 grams)

    ½ cup cooked vegetables such as broccoli or carrot (60 grams)

    1 cup raw leafy vegetables, such as lettuce

■ Fruit – 3 servings

1 serving means: 1 medium orange (200 grams)

    1 medium apple (150 grams)

    ½ punnet strawberries (100 grams)

■ Dairy foods – 2 servings

1 serving means: 300 ml of low-fat milk

    40 grams of low-fat cheese

    200 grams of low-fat yoghurt

■ Meat and alternatives – 1 serving

1 serving means: 120 grams cooked lean beef, veal, lamb or pork

    120 grams lean chicken (raw weight, excluding bone)

    150 grams fish (raw weight, excluding bone)

    2 eggs

    1 cup cooked lentils or dried peas or beans

If you prefer larger servings of meat, go ahead, just make sure it's lean. Protein is a very satiating nutrient.

HOW WELL ARE YOU EATING NOW?

You can check the nutritional quality of your diet yourself. To do this you need a record of your usual food intake. It is ideal if you can keep a food diary of everything you eat and drink for 3–5 days and use this for your assessment.

Remember you have to eat as freely as you normally do, and write down everything – otherwise you're only cheating yourself!

Once you have your total food intake record complete, use the serving size guidelines on pages 38–9 to check you have a balanced intake. The checklists on the following pages can be used to assess your carbohydrate and fat intake.

LOW G.I. EATING

Low G.I. eating means making a move back to the high carbohydrate foods which are staples in many parts of the world, especially whole grains (barley, oats, dried peas and beans) in combination with breads, pasta, vegetables, fruits and certain types of rice.

DO YOU EAT ENOUGH CARBOHYDRATE?

Looking at your diet record and using the serving size guide below estimate the number of servings of carbohydrate foods you had each day. For example, if you had a banana, 2 slices of bread and a medium potato, this counts as 4 servings of carbohydrate.

Carbohydrate food	One serving is	How many did you eat?
Fruit	a handful or 1 medium piece	
Juice	about 1 cup (250 ml)	
Dried fruit	around 1–2 tablespoons	
Bread	1 slice	
Bread roll, bagel	½ a roll, or bagel	
Crackers, crispbread	2 large pieces or 4–6 small crackers	
Rice cakes	2 rice cakes	
Muffin, biscuits	½ a muffin or 2–3 biscuits	
Health bar/sports bar	approximately ½ average bar	
Breakfast cereal	1 bowl or 2 biscuits	
Porridge	about ¼ cup raw oats	
Rice	½ cup of cooked rice	
Pasta, noodles	½ cup of cooked noodles	
Pancakes	about ½ a large pancake	
Burghul, couscous	about ½ cup, cooked	

Carbohydrate food	One serving is	How many did you eat?
Potato, sweet potato	1 medium potato, about 100 grams	
Sweet corn	1 small cob or ½ cup kernels	
Lentils	¾ cup, cooked	
Baked beans, other beans	about ½ cup, cooked	
Total		

Average the number of servings over all the days to come up with a daily average.

Rate yourself:

Less than 4 servings a day	=	Poor.
Between 4 and 8 servings a day	=	Fair, but you need to eat a lot more.
Between 9 and 12 servings a day	=	Good, could need more if you are hungry.
Between 13 and 16 servings a day	=	Great – this should meet the needs of most people.

IS YOUR DIET TOO HIGH IN FAT?

Use this fat counter to tally up how much fat your diet contains. Do a tally for each day and then take an average. Using this fat counter you will need to compare the serving size listed with your serving size and multiply the grams of fat up or down to match your serving size. For example, with milk, if you estimate you might consume 2 cups of regular milk in a day, this supplies you with 20 grams of fat.

Food	Fat content (grams)	How much did you eat?
Dairy Foods		
Milk, (250 ml) 1 cup		
regular	10	
fat-reduced	4	
skimmed	0	
Yoghurt, 200 gram tub		
regular	10	
low-fat	0	
Ice cream, 2 scoops, (100 ml)		
regular	10	
skimmed	3	

Food	Fat content (grams)	How much did you eat?
Cheese		
regular, block cheese,		
30 gram slice	10	
reduced fat block cheese,		
30 gram slice	7.5	
low-fat slices (per slice)	2.5	
cottage, 2 tablespoons	4	
ricotta, 2 tablespoons	4	
Cream/sour cream, 1 tablespoon		
regular	8	
fat reduced	4	
Fats and Oils		
Butter/margarine, 1 teaspoon	4	
Oil, any type, 1 tablespoon, (20 ml)	20	
Cooking spray, per spray	1	
Mayonnaise, 1 tablespoon	7	
Salad dressing, 1 tablespoon	5	
Meat		
Beef		
steak, average, 1 small, lean only	10	
minced beef, 1 cup,(160 grams),		
cooked, drained	15	
sausage, 1 thick, grilled, (80 grams)	14	
topside roast, 2 slices, lean only,		
(80 grams)	4	

Food	Fat content (grams)	How much did you eat?
Lamb		
chump chop, grilled, lean only, 2	9	
leg, roast meat, lean only, 2 slices, (80 grams)	5	
loin chop, grilled, lean only, 2	5	
Pork		
bacon, 1 rasher, grilled	9	
ham, 1 slice, leg, lean	2	
butterfly steak, lean only	5	
leg, roast meat, 3 slices, lean only	4	
loin chop, lean only	4	
Chicken		
breast, skinless	4	
drumstick, skinless	7	
thigh, skinless	7	
½ barbecue chicken (including skin)	15	
Fish		
grilled fish, 1 average fillet	1.5	
salmon, 50 grams	5	
fish fingers, 4 grilled	12	
fish fillets, 2, crumbed, oven baked		
regular	20	
light	10	

Food	Fat content (grams)	How much did you eat?
Snack Foods		
Potato crisps, 50 gram bag	16	
Corn chips, 50 gram bag	14	
Peanuts, ½ cup, (70 grams)	32	
French fries, regular serve	20	
Pizza, 2 slices, medium pizza	25	
Pie/sausage roll	24	
Total		

How did you rate?

Less than 40 grams	=	Excellent. 30 to 40 grams of fat per day is ideal for those trying to lose weight.
41 to 60 grams	=	Good. A fat intake in this range is recommended for most adult men and women.
61 to 80 grams	=	Acceptable. If you are very active, i.e. doing hard physical work (labouring) or athletic training. It is probably too much if you are trying to lose weight.
More than 80 grams	=	You're probably eating too much fat, unless of course you are Superman or Superwoman!

HELPING YOURSELF TO A LOW G.I. DIET

Low fat, low G.I. meal ideas for any time of day.

Breakfast

■ Start with a bowl of low G.I. cereal served with skimmed or low-fat milk or yoghurt

■ Try something like All-Bran™, or rolled oats

■ If you prefer muesli, keep to a small bowl of natural muesli – not toasted

■ Add a slice of toast made from a low G.I. bread (or 2 slices for a bigger person) with a dollop of jam, sliced banana, honey, Marmite, marmalade, or light cream cheese with sliced apple. Keep butter or margarine to a minimum, or use none at all

■ If you like a hot breakfast, try baked beans, a boiled or poached egg, cooked tomatoes or mushrooms with your toast

6 Quick low-fat, low G.I. breakfast ideas

1. Raisin toast spread with fat-reduced cream cheese and topped with sliced apple
2. Porridge made with low-fat milk, sprinkled with raisins and brown sugar

3. A fruit smoothie made with low-fat milk, yoghurt, banana and honey
4. A tub of low-fat yoghurt with a sliced peach and raspberries spooned through
5. Bowl of All-Bran™ and low-fat milk, topped with canned pear slices
6. Baked beans on grainy wholemeal bread

Lunch

■ Try a sandwich or roll, leaving the butter off. If you can, choose a bread with lots of whole grains through it (not just sprinkled on top) for a low G.I. factor

■ For the filling, choose from leg ham, pastrami, lean roast beef or chicken or turkey, or a slice of low-fat cheese, salmon or tuna (in brine), or an egg. An extra container of salad or vegetable soup will help to fill you up

■ Finish your lunch with a piece of fruit, or fruit salad with a low-fat yoghurt, or a low-fat flavoured or plain milk

7 Low G.I. lunches on the Go

1. Take some pitta bread, spread it with hummus, and fill with tabbouleh
2. Chunky vegetable soup, thick with barley, beans and macaroni

3. Boil up a bowl of pasta and mix through pesto or chopped fresh herbs
4. Beat up a banana smoothie and couple it with a high fibre apple muffin
5. Top a tub of fruit salad with a pot of yoghurt
6. Steam or microwave a cob of fresh corn and enjoy as is. Finish with some fruit and yoghurt
7. Take a green salad plus some bean salad, add grainy bread and enjoy

Dinner

■ The basis of dinner should be carbohydrate foods. Take your pick from rice, pasta, potato, sweet potato, couscous, bread, legumes or a mixture

■ Then, add as many vegetables as you can, using a small amount of meat, chicken or fish as a flavouring, rather than the main ingredient

■ Use lean meat, like topside beef, veal, lean pork, trim lamb, chicken breast, fish fillets, turkey. Red meat is a valuable source of iron – just choose lean types. A piece of meat, chicken or fish that fits in the palm of your hand fulfils the daily protein requirements of an adult

- If you prefer not to eat meat, a cup of cooked dried peas, beans, lentils or chick peas can provide protein and iron without any fat. At the same time they supply low G.I. carbohydrate and fibre
- Vegetarian products based on high protein legumes like soya beans and peanuts are good meat alternatives
- Boost your fruit intake and get into the habit of finishing your meal with fruit—fresh, stewed or baked.

7 Low G.I. dinner ideas

1. Team a lean mix of Bolognese sauce (premium beef mince with onions, garlic, tomatoes, celery and carrots) with spaghetti and a green salad
2. Stir-fry chicken, meat or fish with mixed green vegetables. Serve with Basmati rice or Chinese noodles
3. Serve vegetable lasagne with salad
4. Grill a steak and serve with a trio of low G.I. vegetables—new potato, sweet corn and peas
5. Cook spinach and ricotta tortellini with garden vegetables and a tomato and mushroom sauce
6. Wrap a fish fillet dressed with lemon, parsley and garlic in foil. Bake and serve with mixed vegetables or salad
7. Buy a barbecued chicken, steam sweet corn cobs and toss a salad together

7 Quick and easy low G.I. desserts

1. Low-fat ice cream and strawberries
2. Baked whole apple, stuffed with dried fruit
3. Fruit salad with low-fat yoghurt
4. Make a fruit crumble – top cooked fruit with a crumbled mixture of toasted muesli, wheat flakes, a little melted butter and honey
5. Slice a firm banana into some low-fat custard
6. Top canned fruit (peaches or pears) with low-fat ice cream or low-fat custard
7. Wrap pie-packed apple, sultanas, currants and spice, in a sheet of filo pastry (brushed with milk, not fat) and bake as a strudel

SNACKS TO KEEP YOUR ENERGY LEVELS UP BETWEEN MEALS

It's normal to get hungry and eat between meals.

- It is important to include a couple of dairy food servings each day for your calcium needs. If you haven't used yoghurt or cheese in any meals, you may choose to make a low-fat milkshake. One or two scoops of low-fat ice cream or custard can also contribute to daily calcium intake

- If you like grainy breads, an extra slice makes a very good choice for a snack. Other snacks can include a toasted crumpet with a smear of margarine, bagels or fruit loaf

- Fruit is always a low Calorie option for snacks. You should aim to consume at least 3 servings a day. It may be helpful to prepare fruit in advance to make it accessible and easy to eat

- Low-fat crackers (like water crackers) are a low Calorie snack if you want something dry and crunchy, although they may not be as sustaining as a grainy bread. Popcorn (home-prepared with a minimum of fat) is another good alternative

- Keep vegetables (like celery and carrot sticks, baby tomatoes, florets of blanched cauliflower or broccoli) ready prepared

A recent study which compared people eating a diet of three meals a day with those who had three meals and three snacks showed that snacking stimulated the body to use up more energy for metabolism compared with concentrating the same amount of food into three meals. It's as if the more fuel you give your body the more it will burn. Frequent small meals stimulate the metabolic rate.

SUSTAINING SNACKS

Try a muffin	A small tub of low-fat yoghurt
A smoothie	A sandwich
Raisin toast	Dried apricots
A juicy orange	A handful of sultanas
A mini-can of baked beans	A big green apple
A bowl of Sultana Bran™ with low-fat milk	Low-fat ice cream in a cone
	A pile of popcorn (low-fat of course)
A piece of pitta bread and Marmite	

REWARD YOURSELF

If you have been 'good' about your eating all day, reward yourself at the end and enjoy an evening indulgence. Our menus include some suggestions.

10 TIPS FOR COPING WITH CONTROLLING YOUR FOOD INTAKE

- Use hunger as the cue for eating and not the time of day
- Eat a low G.I. carbohydrate food when you are hungry – these foods are the most satiating
- Slow down when you eat to give your stomach a chance to give the signal to your brain that it is full
- When you are thinking about eating, ask yourself how hungry you really are. Delay eating for 30 minutes – true hunger will return
- Don't buy the foods that you don't want to eat
- Indulge in the occasional treat. Lollies are more satiating than chocolates
- Give yourself time to make changes in your habits. It takes about 6 weeks for your tastebuds to readjust
- Once you have served your meal or snack, put the remaining food away, so it is out of sight
- Keep busy during the day
- Don't retrain your food intake excessively – use the eating checklist on pages 38–46 to make sure you eat enough

CHECKLIST OF LOW G.I. FOODS THAT ARE HANDY TO KEEP IN THE CUPBOARD

To make low G.I. choices easy choices, you need to keep the right foods in your pantry.

Breads

If you're the only one in the house who will eat the 'birdseed bread', keep a loaf in the freezer and pull out slices as you need. Choose from these low G.I. breads.

Multigrain breads
Wholemeal breads with Wheatgerm
Pumpernickel
Fruit loaf

Breakfast cereals

All-Bran™ plain
Special K™ (Kellogg)
Natural muesli
Rolled oats

Rice and grains
Pearl barley
Basmati rice
Pasta of various shapes and flavours

Legumes
Pre-cooked and packed lentils, chick peas, split peas
Dried lentils, chick peas, cannellini beans
A variety of canned legumes and pulses (kidney beans,
    mixed beans, baked beans, lentils, chick peas)

Vegetables
Peas
Sweet corn
Sweet potato
Canned new potatoes

Other canned vegetables like tomatoes, asparagus,
peas, mushrooms are handy to boost the vegetable content
of a meal. Buy salt-reduced varieties where possible.
Other convenient products are:
Tomato paste
Tomato purée
Bottled tomato pasta sauces
Frozen vegetables

Fruits

Cherries

Grapefruit

Pears

Apples

Plums

Peaches

Oranges

Grapes

Kiwi-fruit

Dried fruits – sultanas, dried apricots, raisins, prunes etc.

Canned peaches, pears, apple as a useful standby

Dairy foods

Yoghurt – low-fat, fruit and natural

Fat-reduced milks and skimmed milk

UHT skimmed milk or skimmed milk powder – easy to use in cooking

Canned evaporated skimmed milk

Custard powder

Low fat ice-cream

Useful flavourings, sauces and dressings

Spices – curry powder, cumin, turmeric, mustard etc.

Herbs – oregano, basil, thyme etc.

Bottled minced ginger, chilli and garlic

Sauces e.g., soy, chilli, oyster, hoi sin

Stock base (ready prepared) or powders

Low-oil salad dressings

*In our experience of
looking at the diets of people
who want to lose weight
the change needed is sometimes to
eat more, but more of the <u>right</u> foods.*

7 DAYS OF LOW G.I. EATING

Here's a week of healthy, low Calorie menus with all the benefits of low G.I. foods. Each menu is designed to be:

■ **low in fat**

Eating less fat is an easy way to reduce your energy intake. To lose weight we recommend aiming for a daily fat intake of 30–50g. We've used low-fat milk and minimal added fat throughout the menus

■ **high in carbohydrate with a low G.I.**

Carbohydrates, especially those with a low G.I., are the most satisfying for your appetite. It's also the best fuel for your body so we've made sure that at least half the Calories each day come from carbohydrate. This means eating around 200 grams per day as a minimum

■ **low in Calories**

Weight loss will result from a reduction in Calorie intake, but it's important not to go too low. We've aimed for a daily average of 1200–1500 Calories

■ **and nutritionally balanced**

Including a large variety of foods, but in the right proportions, makes you more likely to meet your nutrient needs

These menus are not a prescription! Use them for ideas and as a guide to the amounts and types of foods for a low Calorie diet.

MONDAY

G.I. Factor:	*43*
Total Energy:	*1370 Cal*
Fat:	*29 g*
Carbohydrate:	*226 g*
Fibre:	*32 g*

Breakfast: Rolled oats and fruit

Make up a bowl of porridge using ½ cup raw oats. Top with milk and a sprinkle of sugar and serve with a small glass of orange juice.

or,

Soften the oats for a little while in cold, low-fat milk and eat them like muesli, topped with a sliced banana.

Morning Snack

Handful of dried apricots and a cup of lemon tea

Lunch: Ham and salad sandwich

Skim a little margarine across 2 slices of wholemeal bread, top with a slice of lean ham, tomato, lettuce, grated carrot, beetroot and sprouts. Finish with a juicy apple.

Afternoon Snack
2 oatmeal biscuits with a coffee

Dinner: Vegetarian lasagne and salad
See *The Glucose Revolution* for our low-fat, low G.I.
recipe for Vegetarian Lasagne. Serve with a side salad of
your choice. For dessert, fresh fruit salad and a scoop of
low-fat ice-cream.

Evening indulgence
Fun size (25 g) 'Snickers' (or other) chocolate bar

TUESDAY

G.I. Factor:	*48*
Total Energy:	*1515 Cal*
Fat:	*47 g*
Carbohydrate:	*197 g*
Fibre	*29 g*

Breakfast: Baked beans on toast
Top a slice of grainy toast with a tiny can of
baked beans.
Finish off with a pear or other fresh fruit.

Morning Snack
A small bunch of grapes

Lunch: Soup and bread
Team a bowl of pea and ham soup with a crusty white
bread roll.
Complete the meal with an orange.

Afternoon Snack
Enjoy an iced coffee, made with low-fat milk

Dinner: Spaghetti Bolognaise
See our book, *The Glucose Revolution* for a low-fat, low
G.I. Bolognaise sauce recipe and serve over a cup of
cooked spaghetti. Accompany with a side salad.

Evening indulgence
A small handful of peanuts. If you think you might have
trouble keeping to this, make sure you buy peanuts in the
shell – that will slow you down at least!

WEDNESDAY

G.I. Factor:	47
Total Energy:	1243 Cal
Fat:	20 g
Carbohydrate:	205 g
Fibre:	30 g

Breakfast: Cereal and fruit
½ cup All-Bran™ topped with low-fat milk. Add a piece
of chopped fruit to the cereal or accompany with a small
glass of fruit juice.

Morning Snack
Handful of pretzels

Lunch: Pasta and sauce
Top a cup of boiled pasta with about ⅓ cup of bottled
tomato and mushroom sauce.
Add a mixed leaf salad.

Afternoon Snack
Small, soft serving of low-fat ice cream or fruit ice in a cup or cone

Dinner: Tuna casserole with rice
Make a quick tuna casserole using canned tuna, onion, celery, peas combined in a cheese sauce. Serve with Basmati rice, seasoned with fresh parsley.

Evening Snack
A cup of fresh fruit salad

THURSDAY

G.I. Factor:	*44*
Total Energy:	*1360 Cal*
Fat:	*36 g*
Carbohydrate:	*187 g*
Fibre:	*28 g*

Breakfast: Muesli and yoghurt
Top ½ cup of natural muesli with a little milk, 100 g of 'light' fruit yoghurt and a chopped peach.

Morning Snack
2 oatmeal biscuits and a cup of tea

Lunch: Toasted sandwich
Make a melted cheese & tomato sandwich on toasted grain bread. Finish with a crunchy apple.

Afternoon Snack

Toast a slice of fruit loaf and spread lightly with margarine. Try one of the new 'light' hot chocolate drinks with it.

Dinner: Lamb and vegetables

Grill 2 lean lamb cutlets, basting with a favourite marinade flavouring if desired.

Serve with 3 baby canned new potatoes (steamed or boiled), a small corn cob, broccoli and green beans.

For dessert, have a cup of canned peaches and 2 scoops of low fat ice-cream and finish the meal with a cup of coffee.

FRIDAY

G.I. Factor:	*46*
Total Energy:	*1330 Cal*
Fat:	*30 g*
Carbohydrate:	*190 g*
Fibre:	*28 g*

Breakfast: Tea and toast
½ grapefruit with a teaspoon of sugar followed by 2 slices of grainy bread toast with a light spread of margarine and Marmite and a cup of tea.

Morning Snack
A cup of vegetable soup

Lunch: Jacket potato and beans
Microwave a large potato in its skin until tender. Cut off the top and fill with ⅓ cup baked beans and 1 tablespoon of grated cheese.

Afternoon Snack
A tub of 'diet' yoghurt

Dinner: Beef casserole with mushrooms and wine
Small serving of casserole (containing approximately
100 g cubed meat). Serve with 1 cup of boiled fettucine,
½ cup of green beans and baby carrots.

Evening indulgence
Small packet of potato crisps

SATURDAY

G.I. Factor:	48
Total Energy:	1436 Cal
Fat:	31 g
Carbohydrate:	215 g
Fibre:	22 g

Breakfast: Egg and toast
Small glass of tomato juice, with a boiled egg with a slice of grained bread toast and a second slice with a smear of margarine and marmalade. Tea.

Morning Snack
A crunchy muesli bar

Lunch: Noodles
Make up a packet of quick cook noodles with half the flavour sachet. Add a couple of tablespoons of frozen peas and corn and microwave to heat through.

Afternoon Snack
An ice cream in a cone

Dinner: Fish with lemon and vegetables
Dry cook a 150 g raw fillet of fish, seasoning with lemon juice, and salt and pepper as desired. Serve with a cup of boiled Basmati rice, steamed broccoli and carrots.

Evening Snack
A piece of fresh fruit

SUNDAY

G.I. Factor:	50
Total Energy:	1319 Cal
Fat:	33 g
Carbohydrate:	175 g
Fibre:	27 g

Breakfast: Sunday smoothie
Blend ¾ cup of low-fat milk, 50 g of low-fat natural yoghurt, ½ teaspoon honey, a small banana and a dash of nutmeg in a blender, for a delicious, nourishing drink.

Morning Snack
A slice of Fruit Loaf, toasted, with a smear of margarine

Lunch: Pitta bread pizza
Top a small, wholemeal pitta bread with tomato paste, mushroom, pepper, ham, pineapple, and grated reduced fat cheese. Bake or grill until the cheese melts. Finish up with an apple or orange.

Afternoon Snack
A large bowl of popcorn

Dinner: Steak and salad
Cook a small steak (about 120 g uncooked weight) to your liking. Team with 3 canned baby new potatoes, Mixed Bean Accompaniment (see our book, *The Glucose Revolution,* for a recipe or just use a canned, mixed bean salad) and green salad.

Evening Snack
A generous wedge of melon

HOW TO USE THE G.I. TABLES

These simplified tables are an A to Z listing of the G.I. factor of foods commonly eaten in Britain and the Republic of Ireland. Approximately 300 different foods are listed.

The G.I. value shown next to each food is the average for that food using glucose as the standard, i.e., glucose has a G.I. value of 100, with other foods rated accordingly. The average may represent the mean of 10 studies of that food world wide or only 2 to 4 studies.

We have included some foods in the list which are not commonly eaten (gram dahl) and other foods which may be encountered on overseas trips (e.g. processed breakfast cereals).

To check on a food's G.I., simply look for it by name in the alphabetic list. You may also find it under a food type – fruit, biscuits.

Included in the tables is the carbohydrate (CHO) and fat content of a sample serving of the food. This is to help you keep track of the amount of fat and carbohydrate in your diet. Refer to pages 41 and 43 for advice on how much carbohydrate and fat is recommended.

Remember when you are choosing foods, the G.I. factor isn't the only thing to consider. In terms of your blood sugar levels you should also consider the amount of carbohydrate you are eating. For your overall health the fat, fibre and micronutrient content of your diet is also important. A dietitian can guide you further with good food choices.

If you can't find a G.I. value for a food you eat on many occasions please email us and we'll give you an estimated value of the food and endeavour to test its G.I. in the future. Address your message to:

j.brandmiller@biochem.usyd.edu.au

The G.I. values in these tables are correct at the time of publication. However, the formulation of some commercial foods can change and the G.I. may be altered. Check our web page for revised and new data.
www.biochem.usyd.edu.au/~jennie/GI/glycemic_index.html

A-Z OF FOODS
WITH G.I. FACTOR, PLUS
CARBOHYDRATE & FAT COUNTER

Food	G.I.	Fat	CHO
			(grams per serving)
All Bran™, 40 g	42	1	22
Angel food cake, 30 g	67	trace	17
Apple, 1 medium, 150 g	38	0	18
Apple juice, unsweetened, 250 ml	40	0	33
Apple muffin, 1, 80 g	44	10	44
Apricots, fresh, 3 medium, 100 g	57	0	7
canned, light syrup, 125 g	64	0	13
dried, 5–6 pieces, 30 g	31	0	13
Bagel, 1 white, 70 g	72	1	35
Baked beans, canned in tomato sauce, 120 g	48	1	13
Banana cake, 1 slice, 80 g	47	7	46
Banana, raw, 1 medium, 150 g	55	0	32
Barley, pearled, boiled, 80 g	25	1	17
Basmati white rice, boiled, 180 g	58	0	50
Beetroot, canned, drained, 2–3 slices, 60 g	64	0	5
Bengal gram dhal, 100 g	54	5	57
Biscuits			
Digestives, plain, 2 biscuits, 30 g	59	6	21
Milk Arrowroot, 2 biscuits, 16 g	63	2	13

Food	G.I.	Fat	CHO
			(grams per serving)
Biscuits (*continued*)			
Morning Coffee, 3 biscuits, 18 g	79	2	14
Oatmeal, 3 biscuits, 30 g	54	6	19
Rich Tea, 2 biscuits, 20 g	55	3	16
Shortbread, 2 biscuits, 30 g	64	8	19
Vanilla wafers, 6 biscuits, 30 g	77	5	21
Wheatmeal, 2 biscuits, 16 g	62	2	12
see *also* Crackers			
Black bean soup, 220 ml	64	2	82
Black beans, boiled, 120 g	30	1	26
Black gram, soaked and boiled, 120 g	43	1	16
Blackbread, dark rye, 1 slice, 50 g	76	1	21
Blackeyed beans, soaked, boiled,			
120 g	42	1	24
Blueberry muffin, 1, 80 g	59	8	41
Bran			
Oat bran, 1 tablespoon, 10 g	55	1	7
Rice bran, extruded, 1			
tablespoon, 10 g	19	2	3
Bran Buds™, breakfast cereal, 30 g	58	1	14
Bran muffin, 1, 80 g	60	8	34
Breads			
Dark rye, Blackbread, 1 slice, 50 g	76	1	21
Dark rye, Schinkenbröt, 1 slice,			
50 g	86	1	22

Food	G.I.	Fat	CHO
			(grams per serving)
Breads (*continued*)			
French baguette, 30 g	95	1	15
Fruit loaf, heavy, 1 slice, 35 g	47	1	18
Gluten-free bread, 1 slice, 30 g	90	1	14
Hamburger bun, 1 prepacked bun, 50 g	61	3	24
Light rye, 1 slice, 50 g	68	1	23
Linseed rye, 1 slice, 50 g	55	5	21
Melba toast, 4 squares, 30 g	70	1	19
Pitta bread, 1 piece, 65 g	57	1	38
Pumpernickel, 2 slices	41	2	35
Rye bread, 1 slice, 50 g	65	1	23
Sourdough rye, 1 slice, 50 g	57	2	23
Vogel's™, Honey & Oat loaf, 1 slice, 40 g	55	3	17
White (wheat flour), 1 slice, 30 g	70	1	15
Wholemeal (wheat flour), 1 slice, 35 g	69	1	14
Bread stuffing, 60 g	74	5	17
Breadfruit, 120 g	68	1	17
Breakfast cereals			
All-Bran™, 40 g	42	1	22
Bran Buds™, 30 g	58	1	14
Cheerios™, 30 g	74	2	20

Food	G.I.	Fat	CHO
		(grams per serving)	
Breakfast cereals (*continued*)			
Coco Pops™, 30 g	77	0	26
Cornflakes, 30 g	84	0	26
Mini Wheats™ (whole			
wheat), 30 g	58	0	21
Muesli, toasted, 60 g	43	9	33
Muesli, non-toasted, 60 g	56	6	32
Oat bran, raw, 1 tablespoon,			
10 g	55	1	7
Porridge (cooked with water),			
245 g	42	2	24
Puffed wheat, 30 g	80	1	22
Rice bran, 1 tablespoon, 10 g	19	2	3
Rice Krispies™, 30 g	82	0	27
Shredded wheat, 25 g	67	0	18
Special K™, 30 g	54	0	21
Sultana Bran™, 45 g	52	1	35
Sustain™, 30 g	68	1	25
Weetabix™, 2 biscuits, 30 g	69	1	19
Broad beans, frozen, boiled, 80 g	79	1	9
Buckwheat, cooked, 80 g	54	3	57
Bun, hamburger, 1 prepacked			
bun, 50 g	61	3	24
Burghul, cooked, 120 g	48	0	22
Butter beans, boiled, 70 g	31	0	13

Food	G.I.	Fat	CHO
			(grams per serving)
Cakes			
Angel food cake, 1 slice, 30 g	67	trace	17
Banana cake, 1 slice, 80 g	47	7	46
Flan, 1 slice, 80 g	65	5	55
Pound cake, 1 slice, 80 g	54	15	42
Sponge cake, 1 slice, 60 g	46	16	32
Cantaloupe melon, raw, ¼ small, 200 g	65	0	6
Capellini pasta, boiled, 180 g	45	0	53
Carrots, peeled, boiled, 70 g	49	0	3
Cereal grains			
Barley, pearled, boiled, 80 g	25	1	17
Buckwheat, cooked, 80 g	54	3	57
Burghul, cooked, 120 g	48	0	22
Couscous, cooked, 120 g	65	0	28
Maize			
Cornmeal, wholegrain, cooked, 40 g	68	1	30
Sweet corn, canned, drained, 80 g	55	1	16
Taco shells, 2 shells, 26 g	68	6	16
Millet Ragi, cooked, 120 g	71	0	12
Rice			
Basmati, white, boiled, 180 g	58	0	50
Tapioca (boiled with milk), 250 g	81	10.5	51

Food	G.I.	Fat	CHO
		(grams per serving)	
Cheerios™, breakfast cereal, 30 g	74	2	20
Cherries, 20, 80 g	22	0	10
Chick peas, canned, drained, 95 g	42	2	15
Chick peas, boiled, 120 g	33	3	22
Chocolate, milk, 6 squares, 30 g	49	8	19
Coco Pops™, breakfast cereal, 30 g	77	0	26
Condensed milk, sweetened, ½ cup, 163 g	61	15	90
Corn bran, breakfast cereal, 30 g	75	1	20
Corn chips, Doritos™ original, 50 g	42	11	33
Cornflakes, breakfast cereal, 30 g	84	0	26
Cornmeal (maizemeal), cooked, 40 g	68	1	30
Couscous, cooked, 120 g	65	0	28
Crackers			
Premium soda crackers, 3 biscuits, 25 g	74	4	17
Puffed crispbread, 4 biscuits, wholemeal, 20 g	81	1	15
Rice cakes, 2 cakes, 25 g	82	1	21
Ryvita™, 2 slices, 20 g	69	1	16
Stoned wheat thins, 5 biscuits, 25 g	67	2	17
Water biscuits, 5, 25 g	78	2	18
Croissant, 1	67	14	27

Food	G.I.	Fat	CHO
		(grams per serving)	
Crumpet, 1, toasted, 50 g	69	0	22
Custard, 175 g	43	5	24
Dairy foods			
Ice cream, full fat, 2 scoops, 50 g	61	6	10
Ice cream, low fat, 2 scoops, 50 g	50	2	13
Milk, full fat, 250 ml	27	10	12
Milk, skimmed, 250 ml	32	0	13
Milk, chocolate flavoured, low-fat, 250 ml	34	3	23
Custard, 175 g	43	5	24
Yoghurt			
low-fat, fruit, 200 g	33	0	26
low-fat, artificial sweetener, 200 g	14	0	12
Dark rye bread, Blackbread, 1 slice, 50 g	76	1	21
Dark rye bread, Schinkenbröt, 1 slice, 50 g	86	1	22
Digestive biscuits, 2 plain, 30 g	59	6	21
Doughnut with cinnamon and sugar, 40 g	76	8	16
Fanta™, soft drink, 1 can, 375 ml	68	0	51
Fettucini, cooked, 180 g	32	1	57

Food	G.I.	Fat	CHO
			(grams per serving)
Fish fingers, oven-cooked, 5 × 25 g			
fingers, 125 g	38	14	24
Flan cake, 1 slice, 80 g	65	5	55
French baguette bread, 30 g	95	1	15
French fries, fine cut, small			
serving, 120 g	75	26	49
Fructose, pure, 10 g	23	0	10
Fruit cocktail, canned in natural			
juice, 125 g	55	0	15
Fruit loaf, heavy, 1 slice, 35 g	47	1	18
Fruits and fruit products			
Apple, 1 medium, 150 g	38	0	18
Apple juice, unsweetened, 250 ml	40	0	33
Apricots, fresh, 3 medium, 100 g	57	0	7
canned, light syrup, 125 g	64	0	13
dried, 5–6 pieces, 30 g	31	0	13
Banana, raw, 1 medium, 150 g	55	0	32
Cantaloupe melon, raw,			
¼ small, 200 g	65	0	10
Cherries, 20, 80 g	22	0	10
Fruit cocktail, canned in			
natural juice, 125 g	55	0	15
Grapefruit juice, unsweetened,			
250 ml	48	0	16
Grapefruit, raw, ½ medium, 100 g	25	0	5

Food	G.I.	Fat	CHO
		(grams per serving)	
Fruits and fruit products (*cont.*)			
Grapes, green, 100 g	46	0	15
Kiwifruit, 1 raw, peeled, 80 g	52	0	8
Lychee, canned and drained,			
7, 90 g	79	0	16
Mango, 1 small, 150 g	55	0	19
Orange, 1 medium, 130 g	44	0	10
Orange juice, 250 ml	46	0	21
Pawpaw, ½ small, 200 g	58	0	14
Peach, fresh, 1 large, 110 g	42	0	7
canned, natural juice,			
125 g	30	0	12
canned. heavy syrup,			
125 g	58	0	19
canned, light syrup, 125 g	52	0	18
Pear, fresh, 1 medium, 150 g	38	0	21
canned in pear juice,			
125 g	44	0	13
Pineapple, fresh, 2 slices,			
125 g	66	0	10
Pineapple juice,			
unsweetened, canned,			
250 ml	46	0	27
Plums, 3–4 small, 100 g	39	0	7
Raisins, 40 g	64	0	28

Food	G.I.	Fat	CHO
		(grams per serving)	
Fruits and fruit products (cont.)			
Sultanas, 40 g	56	0	30
Watermelon, 150 g	72	0	8
Gluten-free bread, 1 slice, 30 g	90	1	14
Glutinous rice, white, steamed, 1 cup, 174 g	98	0	37
Gnocchi, cooked, 145 g	68	3	71
Grapefruit juice, unsweetened, 250 ml	48	0	16
Grapefruit, raw, ½ medium, 100 g	25	0	5
Grape Nuts™ cereal, ½ cup, 58g	71	1	47
Grapes, green, 100 g	46	0	15
Green gram dhal, 100 g	62	4	10
Green gram, soaked and boiled, 120 g	38	1	18
Green pea soup, canned, ready to serve, 220 ml	66	1	22
Hamburger bun, 1 prepacked, 50 g	61	3	24
Haricot (navy beans), boiled, 90 g	38	0	11
Honey & Oat Bread (Vogel's™), 1 slice, 40 g	55	3	17
Honey, 1 tablespoon, 20 g	58	0	16
Ice cream, full fat, 2 scoops, 50 g	61	6	10
Ice cream, low-fat, 2 scoops, 50 g	50	2	13
Jelly beans, 5, 10 g	80	0	9

Food	G.I.	Fat	CHO
			(grams per serving)
Kidney beans, boiled, 90 g	27	0	18
Kidney beans, canned and drained, 95 g	52	0	13
Kiwifruit, 1 raw, peeled, 80 g	52	0	8
Lactose, pure, 10 g	46	0	10
Lentil soup, canned, 220 ml	44	0	14
Lentils, green and brown, dried, boiled, 95 g	30	0	16
Lentils, red, boiled, 120 g	26	1	21
Light rye bread, 1 slice, 50 g	68	1	23
Linguine pasta, thick, cooked, 180 g	46	1	56
Linguine pasta, thin, cooked, 180 g	55	1	56
Linseed rye bread, 1 slice, 50 g	55	5	21
Lucozade ™, original, 1 bottle, 300 ml	95	<1	56
Lungkow bean thread, 180 g	26	0	61
Lychee, canned and drained, 7, 90 g	79	0	16
Macaroni cheese, packaged, cooked, 220 g	64	24	30
Macaroni, cooked, 180 g	45	1	56
Maize			
Cornmeal, wholegrain, 40 g	68	1	30
Sweet corn, canned and drained, 80 g	55	1	16

Food	G.I.	Fat	CHO
		(grams per serving)	
Maltose (maltodextrins), pure, 10 g	105	0	10
Mango, 1 small, 150 g	55	0	19
Mars Bar™, 60 g	68	11	41
Melba toast, 4 squares, 30 g	70	1	19
Milk, full fat, 250 ml	27	10	12
Milk, skimmed, 250 ml	32	0	13
chocolate flavoured, 250 ml	34	3	23
Milk, sweetened condensed,			
½ cup, 160 g	61	15	90
Milk Arrowroot biscuits, 2, 16 g	63	2	13
Millet, cooked, 120 g	71	0	12
Mini Wheats™ (whole wheat)			
breakfast cereal, 30 g	58	0	21
Morning Coffee biscuits, 3, 18 g	79	2	14
Muesli bars with fruit, 30 g	61	4	17
Muesli, breakfast cereal			
toasted, 60 g	43	9	33
non-toasted, 60 g	56	6	32
Muffins			
Apple, 1 muffin, 80 g	44	10	44
Bran, 1 muffin, 80 g	60	8	34
Blueberry, 1 muffin, 80 g	59	8	41
Mung bean noodles, 1 cup, 140 g	39	0	35
Noodles, 2-minute, 85 g packet,			
cooked	46	16	55

Food	G.I.	Fat	CHO
		(grams per serving)	
Noodles, rice, fresh, boiled, 1 cup			
176 g	40	0	44
Oat bran, raw, 1 tablespoon, 10 g	55	1	7
Oatmeal biscuits, 3 biscuits, 30 g	54	6	19
Orange, 1 medium, 130 g	44	0	10
Orange juice, 250 ml	46	0	21
Orange squash, diluted, 250 ml	66	0	20
Parsnips, boiled, 75 g	97	0	8
Pasta			
Capellini, cooked, 180 g	45	0	53
Fettucini, cooked, 180 g	32	1	57
Gnocchi, cooked, 145 g	68	3	71
Noodles, 2-minute, 85 g			
packet, cooked	46	16	55
Linguine, thick, cooked, 180 g	46	1	56
Linguine, thin, cooked, 180 g	55	1	56
Macaroni cheese, packaged,			
cooked, 220 g	64	24	30
Macaroni, cooked, 180 g	45	1	56
Noodles, mung bean, 1 cup,			
140 g	39	0	35
Noodles, rice, fresh, boiled,			
1 cup, 176 g	40	0	44
Ravioli, meat-filled, cooked,			
220 g	39	11	30

Food	G.I.	Fat	CHO
			(grams per serving)
Pasta (continued)			
Rice pasta, brown, cooked, 180 g	92	2	57
Spaghetti, white, cooked, 180 g	41	1	56
Spaghetti, wholemeal, cooked, 180 g	37	1	48
Spirale, durum. cooked, 180 g	43	1	56
Star pastina, cooked, 180 g	38	1	56
Tortellini, cheese, cooked, 180 g	50	8	21
Vermicelli, cooked, 180 g	35	0	45
Pastry, flaky, 65 g	59	26	25
Pawpaw, raw, ½ small, 200 g	58	0	14
Pea and ham soup, canned, 220 ml	66	2	13
Peach, fresh, 1 large, 110 g	42	0	7
canned, natural juice, 125 g	30	0	12
canned, heavy syrup, 125 g	58	0	19
canned, light syrup, 125 g	52	0	18
Peanuts, roasted, salted, 75 g	14	40	11
Pear, fresh, 1 medium, 150 g	38	0	21
canned in pear juice, 125 g	44	0	13
Peas, green, fresh. frozen, boiled, 80 g	48	0	5
Peas, dried, boiled, 70 g	22	0	4

Food	G.I.	Fat	CHO
			(grams per serving)
Pineapple, fresh, 2 slices, 125 g	66	0	10
Pineapple juice, unsweetened,			
canned, 250 g	46	0	27
Pinto beans, canned, 95 g	45	0	13
Pinto beans, soaked, boiled, 90 g	39	0	20
Pitta bread, 1 piece, 65 g	57	1	38
Pizza, cheese and tomato, 2 slices,			
230 g	60	27	57
Plums, 3–4 small, 100 g	39	0	7
Popcorn, low-fat (popped), 20 g	55	2	10
Porridge (made with water),			
245 g	42	2	24
Potatoes			
French Fries, fine cut, small			
serving, 120 g	75	26	49
instant potato	83	1	18
new, peeled, boiled, 5 small			
(cocktail), 175 g	62	0	23
new, canned, drained, 5 small,			
175 g	61	0	20
pale skin, peeled, boiled, 1			
medium, 120 g	56	0	16
pale skin, baked in oven (no			
fat), 1 medium, 120 g	85	0	14
pale skin, mashed, 120 g	70	0	16

Food	G.I.	Fat	CHO
			(grams per serving)
Potatoes (continued)			
pale skin, steamed, 1 medium, 120 g	65	0	17
pale skin, microwaved, 1 medium, 120 g	82	0	17
potato crisps, plain, 50 g	54	16	24
Potato crisps, plain, 50 g	54	16	24
Pound cake, 1 slice, 80 g	54	15	42
Pretzels, 50 g	83	1	22
Puffed crispbread, 4 wholemeal, 20 g	81	1	15
Puffed wheat breakfast cereal, 30 g	80	1	22
Pumpernickel bread, 2 slices	41	2	35
Pumpkin, peeled, boiled, 85 g	75	0	6
Raisins, 40 g	64	0	28
Ravioli, meat-filled, cooked, 20 g	39	11	30
Rice			
Basmati, white, boiled, 180 g	58	0	50
Glutinous, white, steamed, 1 cup, 174 g	98	0	37
Instant, cooked, 180 g	87	0	38
Rice bran, extruded, 1 tablespoon, 10 g	19	2	3
Rice cakes, 2, 25 g	82	1	21
Rice Krispies™, breakfast cereal, 30 g	82	0	27

Food	G.I.	Fat	CHO
			(grams per serving)
Rice noodles, fresh, boiled, 1 cup, 176 g	40	0	44
Rice pasta, brown, cooked, 180 g	92	2	57
Rice vermicelli, cooked, 180 g	58	0	58
Rich Tea biscuits, 2, 20	55	3	16
Rye bread, 1 slice, 50 g	65	1	23
Ryvita™ crackers, 2 biscuits, 20 g	69	1	16
Sausages, fried, 2, 120 g	28	21	6
Semolina, cooked, 230 g	55	0	17
Shortbread, 2 biscuits, 30 g	64	8	19
Shredded wheat breakfast cereal, 25 g	67	0	18
Soda crackers, 3 biscuits, 25 g	74	4	17
Soft drink, Coca Cola™, 1 can, 375 ml	63	0	40
Soft drink, Fanta™, 1 can, 375 ml	68	0	51
Soups			
Black bean soup, 220 ml	64	2	82
Green pea soup, canned, ready to serve, 220 ml	66	1	22
Lentil soup, canned, 220 ml	44	0	14
Pea and ham soup, 220 ml	60	2	13
Tomato soup, canned, 220 ml	38	1	15
Sourdough rye bread, 1 slice, 50 g	57	2	23
Soya beans, canned, 100 g	14	6	12

Food	G.I.	Fat	CHO
			(grams per serving)
Soya beans. boiled, 90 g	18	7	10
Spaghetti, white, cooked, 180 g	41	1	56
Spaghetti, wholemeal, cooked, 180 g	37	1	48
Special K™, 30 g	54	0	21
Spirale pasta, durum, cooked, 180 g	43	1	56
Split pea soup, 220 ml	60	0	6
Split peas, yellow, boiled, 90 g	32	0	16
Sponge cake plain, 1 slice, 60 g	46	16	32
Sports drinks			
Gatorade, 250 ml	78	0	15
Isostar, 250ml	70	0	18
Stoned wheat thins, crackers, 5 biscuits, 25 g	67	2	17
Sucrose, 1 teaspoon	65	0	5
Sultana Bran™, 45 g	52	1	35
Sultanas, 40 g	56	0	30
Sustain™, 30 g	68	1	25
Swede, peeled, boiled, 60 g	72	0	3
Sweet corn, 85 g	55	1	16
Sweet potato, peeled, boiled, 80 g	54	0	16
Sweetened condensed milk, ½ cup, 160 g	61	15	90
Taco shells, 2, 26 g	68	6	16

Food	G.I.	Fat	CHO
		(grams per serving)	
Tapioca pudding, boiled with milk, 250 g	81	10.5	51
Tapioca, steamed 1 hour, 100 g	70	6	54
Tofu frozen dessert (non-dairy), 100 g	115	1	13
Tomato soup, canned, 220 ml	38	1	15
Tortellini, cheese, cooked, 180 g	50	8	21
Vanilla wafer biscuits, 6, 30 g	77	5	21
Vermicelli, cooked, 180 g	35	0	45
Waffles, 25 g	76	3	9
Water biscuits, 5, 25 g	78	2	18
Watermelon, 150 g	72	0	8
Weetabix™ breakfast cereal, 2 biscuits, 30 g	69	1	19
Wheatmeal biscuits, 2, 16 g	62	2	12
White bread, wheat flour, 1 slice, 30 g	70	1	15
Wholemeal bread, wheat flour, 1 slice, 35 g	69	1	14
Yakult, 65 ml serve	46	0	11
Yam, boiled, 80 g	51	0	26
Yoghurt			
low-fat, fruit, 200 g	33	0	26
low-fat, artificial sweetener, 200 g	14	0	12

WHERE TO GO FOR HELP AND FURTHER INFORMATION

Dietitians

State Registered Dietitians (SRDs) are nutrition experts who can provide nutritional assessment and guidance and support with weight loss. Check for SRD. Glycaemic index is part of their training so all dietitians should be able to help in applying principles in this guide, but some dietitians do specialise. If you want more detailed advice on glycaemic index just check with the dietitian when booking.

For a list of dietitians in your area contact the British Dietetic Association or the Irish Nutrition & Dietetic Institute.

It is also worth checking in the Yellow Pages for your area, under Dietitians.

Numerous community support groups which can encourage and motivate, usually for a nominal fee.

If seeking the services of a commercial weight loss organisation, check that they comply to expected standards.

British Diabetic Association
10 Queen Anne Street
London W1M 0BD
Telephone: 0207 323 1531

British Dietetic Association
5th Floor, Elizabeth House
22 Suffolk Street Queensway
Birmingham B1 1LS
Telephone: 0121 616 4900

Irish Nutrition & Dietetic Institute
Dundrum Business Centre
Frankfort Dundrum
Dublin 14
Ireland
Telephone: (1) 298 7466

ABOUT THE AUTHORS

Kaye Foster-Powell, an accredited practising dietitian-nutritionist, has extensive experience in diabetes management and has researched practical applications of the glycaemic index. She is the senior dietitian at Wentworth Area Diabetes Service and conducts a private practice in the Blue Mountains, New South Wales. Her most recent book is the best-selling *Glucose Revolution*, published by Hodder & Stoughton.

Associate Professor Jennie Brand Miller, a senior member of the teaching and research staff of the Human Nutrition Unit at the University of Sydney, is a world authority on the glycaemic index of foods and its applications to diabetes. Her most recent book is the best-selling *Glucose Revolution*, published by Hodder & Stoughton.

Dr Stephen Colagiuri, Director of the Diabetes Centre and Head of the Department of Endocrinology, Metabolism and Diabetes at the Prince of Wales Hospital in Randwick, New South Wales, has published extensively on the importance of carbohydrate in the diet of people with diabetes. His most recent book is the best-selling *Glucose Revolution*, published by Hodder & Stoughton.